Setting Career Goals

by Stuart Schwartz and Craig Conley

Content Consultant:
Robert J. Miller, Ph.D.
Associate Professor
Mankato State University

CAPSTONE
HIGH/LOW BOOKS
an imprint of Capstone Press

C A P S T O N E   P R E S S

818 North Willow Street • Mankato, MN 56001
http://www.capstone-press.com

Library of Congress Cataloging-in-Publication Data
Schwartz, Stuart, 1945-
    Setting career goals/by Stuart Schwartz and Craig Conley
    p. cm. -- (Life skills)
    Includes bibliographical references and index.
    Summary: Provides an introduction to assessing skills, exploring options, and
setting goals in the workplace.
    ISBN 1-56065-722-7
    1. Life skills--Juvenile literature. 2. Career development--Juvenile literature.
[1. Life skills. 2. Career development.] I. Conley, Craig, 1965- . II. Title. III. Series:
Schwartz, Stuart, 1945- Life skills.
HQ2037.S283 1998
646.7--dc21   97-51300
                                                  CIP
                                                  AC

Photo credits:
All photos by Dede Smith Photography

Table of Contents

Chapter 1

Why Set Career Goals?

Setting career goals helps workers get better jobs. A goal is an objective that a person tries to accomplish.

Some people stay in one career throughout their lives. Others work at many careers to reach their career goals.

For example, a restaurant cashier may want to become a restaurant manager. A manager is a person in charge of a business or department. The cashier learns to cook, serve food, and clear tables. Learning these skills may help the worker become a manager. It may help the cashier reach a career goal.

Setting career goals takes planning. Workers who set career goals think about their skills. They decide what kinds of work they want to do. They learn what training they need. They find out if they should go to school. They set their goals. Then they work hard to reach those goals.

Setting career goals takes planning.

Chapter 2

Opportunities at Work

Workers can look for opportunities where they work. They can learn about other jobs within companies. They can find out which skills they need for other jobs.

Workers can learn about other jobs by talking to co-workers. For example, an office worker at a school may want to be a teacher. The office worker can ask teachers about the skills they need. The office worker can also find out what training teachers need.

Most companies have personnel offices. Companies hire and pay workers through personnel offices. These offices have listings of jobs that are available within companies. Workers can go to personnel offices to learn about the jobs. Then they can apply for the available jobs.

Workers can learn about other jobs from co-workers.

Chapter 3

Discovering Skills

Workers can plan their careers by discovering their skills. They can discover their skills by taking skills tests. The tests are not hard. Test results show workers their strengths and weaknesses. They show which kinds of jobs workers might do well.

For example, a typist takes a skills test. The typist might learn that he or she has strong writing skills. The typist can learn about jobs for people with writing skills.

Workers can take skills tests at some personnel offices. Schools offer skills tests. Workers can take skills tests at employment agencies. An employment agency is a business that helps workers find jobs.

Workers can also learn about their interests by taking tests. Interest tests help workers discover the kinds of jobs they might enjoy. Workers usually want to find jobs that combine their interests and their skills.

Workers can discover their skills by taking skills tests.

Chapter 4

Learning about Jobs

Successful people often learn about many jobs before they set career goals. This helps them make better decisions.

Workers can learn about jobs at employment agencies or personnel offices. They can also learn by talking to people who work in different jobs.

Workers can learn how much training they will need to meet their career goals. For example, a factory worker might learn how much training is needed to become a supervisor. A supervisor is a person who is in charge of workers.

Workers can find out how much money they can earn for certain jobs. They can learn which jobs may lead to better jobs. For example, an applicant can ask whether a store clerk position could lead to a job as a manager. An applicant is a person who applies for something.

Learning about jobs helps workers know what they want. It helps them prepare to set career goals.

Workers can learn about jobs at personnel offices.

Chapter 5

Reaching Goals

Workers who reach career goals know which jobs they want. They work hard to earn these jobs.

Education is important. Workers need a high school education for many jobs. For example, postal workers must have a high school education. Workers need a college education for other jobs. College is a school people go to after high school. For example, nurses need a college education.

Workers may need experience for some jobs. For example, a restaurant manager may want cooks with three years of cooking experience. Sometimes experience in the same kind of workplace is helpful. The manager may consider an applicant who worked as a cook's helper. As a helper, the applicant may have learned a lot about being a cook.

Workers need licenses for some jobs. A license is official permission to do a job. For example, child care workers and hair stylists often need licenses. Workers usually go to school or take special training to earn licenses.

Child care workers often need licenses.

Chapter 6

Steps to Success

Successful people reach their career goals one step at a time. Many successful people make lists of the steps necessary to reach their goals. The lists help them remember what to do next.

Suppose a person wants to be a barber. He or she makes a list of the steps needed to become a barber. The first step is earning a high school diploma or passing a GED test. A GED test measures knowledge of high-school subjects. A person who passes the test earns a GED certificate. Earning this certificate is equal to finishing high school.

Next the person must attend a barber school. The person learns how to cut hair at a barber school. Then the person must apply for a license. The license allows the person to get a job cutting hair.

Finally, the person gets a job as a barber. The person has reached a career goal.

People who reach goals know that each step takes time. They allow themselves enough time to complete each step.

Many successful people make lists of the steps necessary to reach their goals.

Chapter 7

Finding Help

It is not always easy to set goals. People may need to ask for help. Others can help them learn to set goals.

People can go to employment agencies for help. Workers in employment agencies offer career advice. They explain the training needed for jobs. They may help people receive the training they need.

People must pay for services at most employment agencies. Many states have job service agencies. A job service agency is a government office that offers career advice and help finding jobs. Their services are often free.

People can learn from successful workers. For example, a typist can ask an office manager for advice. The typist can ask about becoming a manager. The manager can help the typist learn how to reach goals.

Students can ask school counselors for help. A school counselor is a person trained to give students advice. Workers can get similar advice from people who work in personnel offices.

People can go to employment agencies for help.

Chapter 8

Improving Skills

Successful workers look for chances to improve. They know they can reach career goals by improving their skills. Some workers improve the skills they already have. Others learn new skills.

Workers can learn from supervisors. A supervisor may offer advice about how to improve job skills.

Workers can improve their skills by receiving training. They can take classes. For example, cooks can attend classes on preparing foods. Office workers can take classes to improve their computer skills.

Workers can improve skills in other ways. Speaking at meetings improves public speaking skills. Being a leader of work teams or groups outside of work improves leadership skills.

Workers who improve their skills show they want to succeed. They are taking steps toward reaching their career goals.

Workers who improve their skills show they want to succeed.

Chapter 9

Learning from Mistakes

All workers make mistakes. Successful workers learn from their mistakes. Learning helps them reach their career goals. They learn not to repeat mistakes.

For example, a shipping clerk sends orders to customers. A customer is a person who buys something. The clerk puts the wrong address on one order. The customer does not receive the order. The clerk decides to check addresses carefully on future orders. The clerk has learned from the mistake.

Sometimes supervisors see workers make mistakes. Good supervisors show workers how to avoid future mistakes. Smart workers learn from their supervisors.

Workers can also help each other. They can share information about how to avoid making common mistakes.

Successful workers learn from their mistakes.

Chapter 10

Being Flexible

Flexible workers know they may have to change their plans in order to reach goals. Flexible means willing to change.

Many things can cause workers to change their career plans. Workers might find jobs in other companies. They may get promotions. A promotion is a better, higher-paying job. Sometimes workers move to other cities to join family members.

Flexible workers find new ways to reach goals. Suppose a fast-food worker is saving money for college. The worker takes a job with a different company. The company will pay for the worker to go to college. The worker makes a new career plan.

Successful workers find many ways to reach their goals. They change their plans when their jobs or their lives change. But their goals often remain the same.

Flexible workers find many ways to reach their career goals.

Chapter 11

Rewarding Progress

Workers take many steps to reach their goals. They can keep track of their progress by crossing steps off their lists. Some steps are small. Other steps are big. Each step brings workers closer to their goals.

Workers can reward themselves for completing steps toward a goal. Workers who reward themselves feel better about their work. They work harder. They keep working toward their goals. Then they can reward themselves again.

Workers can reward themselves by doing activities they enjoy. For example, an office worker completes a project. The worker goes out to dinner with family members. This is the worker's reward. A truck driver completes college. The truck driver's reward is taking a special vacation.

Workers can reward themselves for reaching goals.

Chapter 12

Career Goals and You

Setting career goals can help you succeed in the workplace. Setting goals will help you take the right steps toward your main goal.

Talk to others to learn about jobs that you might enjoy. Find out about the training you may need for these jobs. You can also learn about your skills and interests by taking tests.

Know the steps you must take to earn the job you want. You may need more education. You may need more experience. List each step. This will help you plan.

You will find many ways to reach career goals. You can ask people for help. You can improve your skills. You can learn from your mistakes. It is important to reward yourself for each successful step you take.

Reaching career goals is hard work. But knowing what you want to accomplish can lead you to a successful career.

Setting career goals can help you succeed.

Words to Know

employment agency (em-PLOI-muhnt AY-juhn-see)—a business that helps workers find jobs

flexible (FLEK-suh-buhl)—willing to change

goal (GOHL)—an objective a person tries to accomplish

job service agency (JOB SUR-viss AY-juhn-see)—a government office that offers career advice and help finding jobs

license (LYE-suhnss)—official permission to do a job

promotion (pruh-MOH-shuhn)—a better, higher-paying job

school counselor(SKOOL COUN-suh-lur)—a person trained to give students advice

supervisor (SOO-pur-vye-zur)—a person who is in charge of workers

To Learn More

McFarland, Rhoda. *The World of Work*. New York: Rosen Publishing Group, 1993.

Milios, Rita. *Discovering How to Make Good Choices*. New York: Rosen Publishing Group, 1992.

Smith, Sandra Lee. *Setting Goals*. New York: Rosen Publishing Group, 1992.

Useful Addresses

Adult Education/Training Information Service
325 Queens Avenue
London, Ontario N6B 1X2
Canada

National Center on Adult Literacy
University of Pennsylvania
3910 Chestnut Street
Philadelphia, PA 19104

U.S. Department of Education
Office of Vocational and Adult Education
4090 MES
330 C Street SW
Washington, DC 20202

Internet Sites

Career Web
http://www.cids.org.za/sa_careers/
  ten-main.htm

Planning a Career: A Guided Tour
http://adventuresineducation.org/
  adventur/planning.htm

Self-Assessment
http://www.bsu.edu/careers/selfases.html

The Training Information Source
http://www.training-info.com/

Index